Tuckasee

poems by

B.J. Wilson

Finishing Line Press
Georgetown, Kentucky

Tuckasee

Copyright © 2020 by B.J. Wilson
ISBN 978-1-64662-225-2 First Edition
All rights reserved under International and Pan-American Copyright Conventions. No part of this book may be reproduced in any manner whatsoever without written permission from the publisher, except in the case of brief quotations embodied in critical articles and reviews.

ACKNOWLEDGMENTS

Several of the poems in this collection originally appeared in the following journals:

"Herons" in *The Jefferson Review*
"The Field" and "Species Composition" in *New Madrid*
"Main Street Blues" in *Notations*

I would also like to thank the Bluegrass Writers Studio at Eastern Kentucky University, especially my professors, Julie Hensley and Young Smith, and all my classmates, specifically, Steve Cambron, Maryelizabeth Pope, and Richard Stuecker, for their feedback on many of these poems. I also want to thank my friend, Dan Dietrich, for reading versions of these poems (and all the poems over the years). I would lastly like to thank Richard Stuecker, once again, for his help finalizing this manuscript, the encouragement to keep writing, and above all, his friendship.

Publisher: Leah Maines
Editor: Christen Kincaid
Cover Art: Yves Moret
Author Photo: Kim Byram
Cover Design: Russell Helms

Printed in the USA on acid-free paper.
Order online: www.finishinglinepress.com
also available on amazon.com

Author inquiries and mail orders:
Finishing Line Press
P. O. Box 1626
Georgetown, Kentucky 40324
U. S. A.

Table of Contents

Banding Geese with the Tennessee Wildlife Resource Agency 1

Birds are Just Gloried Reptiles 2

Killing a Cottonmouth 3

The Natural Selection 5

One Last Look at the Foxes 6

Heronry 7

Herons 8

Species Composition 9

Fieldwork 10

Energy Lake 13

The Field 21

Black Puma 22

For Snyder 23

Main Street Blues 24

Notes 25

for my parents

And grass, grass, blossom through my feet in flames.

—Galway Kinnell

Banding Geese with the Tennessee Wildlife Resource Agency

Mobs of molting Canada geese hiss
      and flash their purple

slug tongues, slash with webbed feet
      that cut, fifty with me

in the makeshift pen. I'm told to grab
      each one by its neck,

tuck the head under one of the wings
      to calm it down

under the dark. Instead, I dig through
      the downy frenzy—

gray feathers afloat like ashes—
      for the one trampled on its side

unmoving, blood damp in the white
      of its breast feathers.

I slide my hands underneath it,
      take dead weight into my arms.

Then it awakens against my chest!
      We love each other.

But it must flail its wings, this wild
      wriggling mass I hand

to the next technician, who'll pass it
      along to the old timer,

plump under the tarp in a fold-out chair,
      a streak of dried blood,

I'm not sure whose, across his forearm,
      a goose asleep in his lap.

Birds are Just Glorified Reptiles

Another night heron flew through my rib cage and left behind
its reflection, but no one ever wades into a slough with an alligator.

When I thought she might have wanted me, I shot my load
over my shoulder, but she was only interested in my shoulder's leaves.

A Southern copperhead winds across the top of my waitress' breasts.
Calling from the reeds, boy red-winged black birds spread their tails.

One night, alone in his room, a drunk Jesse James pistoled holes
into the tavern's wall because of the pattern of birds on the curtains.

Killing a Cottonmouth

Once the dust
    on the dirt road
        clears,
the split,
    pink flesh
        glistens—
Allen couldn't
    cut the truck
        in time.
Chris is quick
    to pin its head
        with PVC,
dig his heel
    into its skull,
        and back away.
But like a cobra,
    the cottonmouth
        rises,
to bear the pearl
    of its mouth
        to the world.
Instead, by
    ligaments
        its lower jaw
hangs like
    an open
        gallows door.
Like my finger
    severed by
        an ice skate
when my hands
    had to break
        the fall:

just a red ring
        at first
                until it slid
to the side,
        held only
                by a tendon,
and after
        lifting it up,
                clamping
it back,
        I passed out.

In the seconds
        it takes to grab
                a hatchet
and a hammer,
        Chris has
                finished it—
dust like
        the viper
                his testament.
Where would
        my mind
                have been?
We each take
        Copenhagen for our
                lower lips,
the ride back and
        a quiet no one
                would disturb.

The Natural Selection

The weasel hunted all the barn rats in my hayricks, a total of seventeen in a pile it left on the hill, meat which it'll cache below the ground.

The weasel won't suck blood like some think, though they'll lop it up given the chance: when there's a surplus kill, they eat the brains first.

The weasel was born in winter, kin to badger, wolverine. Winds like a snake through a vole's own tunnel of snow, corners it in its own den.

The weasel does indeed have a war dance: they flop and twirl and spin, inching toward the hare the whole damn time. Some just die by fright.

The weasel won't release its bite with its prey writhing, even into the air. Eleven of them came after me. Evolution could have rooted that out.

One Last Look at the Foxes

Where the Regional Economic Development Center
now stands, there once stood
a little wooded lot with a stream.
The university's grounds crew
had a mulch pile nearby,

where we'd shovel up the truck after planting.
Once, three red fox pups popped up
above that mulch pile, right in a row,
too young to worry about us.
When I had some time

to kill, I took the most careful green steps
into their midday darkness.
I wasn't the one to displace them—
I found the foxes with their mother
practicing balance on a log.

Heronry

1.
Walking along the Tennessee again, I am reminded
    of how cottonwood leaves tremble

with little wind, the poison ivy always quick to get
    to the shoestrings then the hands.

A mud stained mattress half hides in green shade.
    A *Quasar* television farther down

in the weeds, rusted, its broken screen all caved in.
    A carp floats bellyup in the cove.

Then three great blue herons drawn from wet brush
    as if I'd stumbled upon a rookery,

the green shoreline far too dense for me to tell.
    Another heron's wide wingbeats cut

into the heat, carry my gaze, sleepily, over the river
    toward a parked barge full of coal.

2.
I wanted to show her a trail I'd found, down a slough
    thick with stands of bald cypress,

black willow, and button bush. Where I'd seen
    a green heron perched in a tupelo.

But she was more drawn to a gravestone, covered now
    in day lilies, fronds in wild disarray,

orange blooms below names carved into the stone—
    husband and wife, born in the 1860s,

but however hard I try to find it, in green leaf and vine,
    the old trail here is just as buried.

Herons
after Elizabeth Bishop

High above the spillway,
sunlight flicks off windshields
of cars crossing the dam.
The towering cranes,
backhoes and dump trucks,
and company SUVs
for bridge building rest
squat and unattended—
it's my lunch break too.
No trolling john boats
or smoke-snorting tugs,
just five great blue herons
scattered on the riprap
looking for handouts.
These tall and lanky,
solitary waders of the sloughs
one by one come closer.
Sandwich in hand,
I rise and throw my arms
in the air as their wide wings
open, the blue afternoon!

Species Composition

Our motorboat   pounds, thrusts   against winds,
and breaks through lake waves—plummets
hard, over and over   for two and a half hours.

Pewter water   swells, almost molten, like mercury,
clustered auburn crowns of the shorelines   like rust.
Blurred   and vast,   the masked sun
behind gray   glares with a film   like platinum.

The bow   crashes, throttle   out of gear again.
My uncle tugs the motor's chord again, and sways
ankle-deep in the stern's pool   while lake wind
whips his doused clothes.

Traps set for measuring the lake island's mammals
yield a marsh rice rat, a white-footed mouse,
which we measure, weigh, and release.

And a raccoon, hiding under a husk
it made from twigs and leaves—
silver tufts of fur bulge from the cage.

That's a big coon, my uncle says, then disappears
among trees, to find a stick long enough
to safely set it free.

In the quiet   the raccoon stirs   finally shows its face,
peering upward   through the bars   from debris
it gathered with its hands   from inside the cage
like a kid covering himself   in the sand.

Its tired   mammalian eyes, like   mine, gaze deeply,
as yellow lanceolate leaves blow between us.

Fieldwork

> *Between my finger and my thumb*
> *The squat pen rests.*
> *I'll dig with it.*
>   —Seamus Heaney

1.
Each day we eat our lunches on the logs
    far from the trails. Shadows of egrets

slip across my boots into the swamp grass,
    but in the bottomlands, you hear as much

as you see: red-shouldered hawks
    cry out in afternoon, the barred owl's

call like a spell in the evening;
    before you can see them, deer bound

deeper into the green-dark, crashing through
    undergrowth, more real than hoofprints.

And you have to watch for cottonmouths—
    your step, where you put your hands.

Allen shoulders his backpack, vanishes
    into the brush: lunch is over. My pack,

tightened at the chest, weighs me down,
    as I fumble with an auger bit that takes

two hands to hold. Shit gets slick in the silt,
    greenbrier, Virginia creeper, trumpet vine—

ground cover that could twist a boot into
    a tumble, a would-be crunch onto blades.

2.
Allen is a scientist. For his measurements
>he calibrates a truckload of equipment.

Adept in his estimates, he can calculate
>a tree's worth, a quick figure, talk shop

with peer PhD candidates like James who's
>studying beavers at the Ames plantation

where he lives in an old overseer's house
>he claims is haunted. (From Mississippi,

he figures that Tennessee has no business
>pretending to belong to the South.)

When Allen has me measure the diameter
>of old growth trunks roped in poison oak,

I'm forced to turn aside to keep the leaves
>from my face. Hasn't he seen me crush

the jewel weed into a syrup for my skin?
>And when he sends me waist deep into

a corner of a creek, where a cottonmouth's
>just slithered in, I'm fearful of the power

behind its poison. *That'll be all,* he says,
>shaving, after a reprimand at the house.

3.
Today we bushwhack: Allen on his ATV,
        Chris and I on foot with our machetes

through multiflora rose, wild blackberry,
        cottonwood and ash saplings and cane.

Today our gear's in the canoe, so we wade,
        careful not to let water from the sloughs

into our waders, of drowning in American
        lotus, wild iris, water lily, and duckweed.

Today we run the auger several feet deep
        down into the silt and draw blue clay,

set PVC pipe, until I find a fawn curled
        in jewel weed, new enough to cup in hands,

bright orange and brown and dappled in dots,
        the three of us around it as if it were a fire.

The mother has left it bedded so she can feed.
        We know she watches from the green-dark.

We hear her silence held within the canopy
        like a breath, all of us held within her gaze—

white-eyed vireo, towhee, Kentucky warbler,
        a sudden flock of fish crows, wing and call.

Energy Lake

Invocation

Barred owl perched
    on a branch in the day-dark
of the marsh—
    would you
allow us through the arrow arum?

1.
Before my grandmother died, she spoke to me of her kin, a man named McCauley from Scotland, who passed the teacher's exam and set up a post office with so much energy, that that's what they called it, Energy. Then she put back his black and white photograph in the roll top desk. The TVA flooded that land, many times, Energy under its water now.

Four days, three nights on
    the North-South Trail,
Energy Lake nearly to my nose,
    sunset's water wavering
on my eyelids, my eyes closed.

    o

Green treefrog's toes
    stuck to the campground store
glass door, for twilight's mosquitoes
    wooed by false light.
I've already mopped the floor,

sold a permit—shot shit—
    sold popsicles to Maintenance
breaking from the heat. And I've
    already cleaned campsites,
found a rat snake winding through ash.

2.
My first memory of western Kentucky: my uncle drove his canoe to Ferguson Spring, which I kept calling Emerson Spring, by mistake, once I came to work in its forest. We put in downstream from a beaver dam, the lodge thick with sticks. Snuck up on a buck in his crimson summer coat—he'd nowhere to go as we slid by, paddling the creeks into the open American lotus of Energy Lake.

Veering off the Western Kentucky
    Parkway, my granddad bashed in
his hood, then everyone else woke too.
    You hit the floor or something,
mom says, when I ask. *You were four.*

o

I either hiked upland forest with Kevin for openings in the conifers, GPS the size of a lawnmower motor attached to the tip of a pole long as a broom, or followed Mara through the swamp rice grass, dark flash of a rat snake over my boot back into the green and gone on the first day. Waded through sloughs in the bottoms of Emerson Spring, a pair of hands for her thesis, constructing transects, recording measurements. Tugged tape over my shoulder, water just below my waders—one technician drowned in a slough, she warned. Our decomposition nurtures the ground, she told me, which wasn't a warning for her. Where do *you* think *you* go when *you* die? she'd asked.

Yellow-crowned night heron
    clambering into the warm
morning air, yellow legs
    just above the slough,
its tassel trailing like a shadow.

3.
Kevin's old lady Tracy gave me a ride to the bus station in Mayfield. Had to hit Memphis on the way to Georgia—three-hour layover no AC, ambulance and police outside. A man wanted to show me to a shelter. Beale Street on a weekday afternoon means everybody's white, won't serve a white man with a shitty rucksack and a beard, so no trophy gumbo to try. *Denny's* on a weekday means everybody's black, waitresses giddy over Bow Wow in town, his A&R in a headset picking up patty melts. Passed a detention center in Georgia, boys like pines.

Kev living in an RV, taking measurements,
    riding around Okefenokee
in an ATV. On his off time back in the swamp
    with a stave, lifting logs
and bark for snakes: corn, king, and canebrake.

        o

From the tower, little blue heron—
    purple and lavender
up close in the sweat-wet
    set of Kev's binoculars,
—guarding the wet savannah.

        o

Maritime forest live oaks
    drip days
after the rain, sky half-purpled,
    half-blacked, wild
horses' shit in the sand dunes.

4.
Brown pelicans in the estuary
        crash into fish—
no manatee or dolphin,
        just pelican & cormorant,
white egret wings off

above the mangroves and islands
        heavy-nested & off
limits: no trails, no trace.

                o

        White ibis back in a bayou,
the curvature of its bill a secret.

                o

After an egret through saw palmetto
        and pine. Hide outstretched
on a bed of pine needles
        and sand. Wait
each other out in the shade, cool

ocean wind in from the Gulf. Camp
        on the beach, wake
to dolphins way out on the waves.
        And I'm
not drunk this time.

5.

Crossing a cottonfield, I catch a colony of white Mississippi kites above the treetops near the Hatchie. Stepping between hard, summered furrows, I slip into the woodline—scarlet cardinal flowers, orange jewel weed, wild black berry by the braided brooks. Fat swamp rabbit on its hind legs, gorging berries like a bear cub, dives into the creek, drifts underwater like an otter.

Haul PVC pipe deep through the silt, burrow the auger three feet into the silt, plant PVC pipe deep into the silt. Calibrate an instrument, monitor the sediment, cottonwoods trembling like aspen.

Zazen before bed on the mat
    where I sleep: dream across
cottonfields into a woodline's
    green shade.

o

A cottonmouth coiled
    in the heavy summer heat
warms its amber skin.
    Days after the storm-tear,
the bottom is groggy and still,

the brown river high—sheets spilt
    across the floodplain
have ponded the willow and cypress.
    Cottonwood seeds drift
sunlit, weightless in the afternoon.

6.
Radioed in: *I'm checking trails . . . holler if you need me.* After a summer tanager through forest, off trail, tree after tree. We do this for a while, he and I. Back on Cherokee Trail, down a switchback to the lakeshore's buttonbush, eyes wide for cottonmouths, fish-eagles and osprey.

Hopped out the park truck
    to help a turtle
from the road—big & bronze
    spiked dragon tail
& shell: put your hands

on a snapping turtle &
    you're bound
to get hissed at, probably
    bit, but I got
lucky, now, lucky as shit—

left that guy where he was,
    went to climb
back into my own shell, Rachel
    shining, laughing
behind the windshield.

                o

That's spice bush. If you crush it,
    it'll smell like *Fruity Pebbles.*
That's sassafras: they use it
    to make root beer. Does everyone
like root beer? *Yesssssssssssss!*

That's white oak: *quercus alba*.
        Watch for momma raccoon
and her babies. (But what kids
        dug most: dead leopard frogs I'd pull
from the skimmer at the state park pool.)

                Benediction

We come looking for
        the Temple of Flying Petals,
making the most
        of the light that's left.
—*Su Tung-P'o.*

7.
My wildlife biology roommates are laughing as dusk comes to the Crooked Creek Bay boat dock, just the other side of Energy Lake Dam, and I don't know what's so funny all these years away. But I remember lightning, a quick wind in the oncoming night, and laughter as if we could've cared less. On the way out of Land Between the Lakes, we would've watched, like always, for snakes and frogs drawn to the warm roads—a Southern copperhead Nick once dinged with his *Bronco*, blood out the side of its mouth, red against pink skin glowing in the headlights, all of us encircled and solemn and in awe.

Now, from the same dock, I watch fish alight, three or four at a time, from the gold-green—trees and a late sun shimmering on the water. I've forgotten so many of the names: grasses, a sedge from a reed, herbaceous plants at the lake-bank. Whole stands of trees. A bird blue and rouge too big for a swallow.

Leaving Energy Lake, the service roads widen, and trees which arched over on the way in ease back gently into meadows,

but not before an offering—
      a prothonotary warbler
nicked off the windshield:
      a trace of gold like the bar
of sunset through trees.

The Field

My grandfather spent several years
in a nursing home
before he died, the curtain of memory
drawn steadily in that pale,
pea green room, until he lost
all remembrance,
and I became a shadow by his bedside.

At a cottonfield's edge one summer,
facing the dark emerald
world beyond the woodline,
I remembered him
the way heat lightning will flicker
at night and illuminate the unseen.

From the darkness of my mind
my grandfather
reaching from the darkness of his own—

telling me by his bedside in a moment
of recognition that he loved me,
rasp of his voice, his hand
clasping my elbow: the electrical surge.

Black Puma

On his way to work
at the plant
my uncle saw it
leap from the backroad—
a black flash
over the roadside
at dawn.

When I was older,
I heard him
educe its color, allow
that *things look darker
in the half-light.*

It is an onyx
gliding toward trees
into the dense, boyish
darkness of the forest.

For Snyder

He read from his new haibun,
praised the evening light of a west Tennessee trail
he made time to hike:

southeast green & gold
walk on through.

    We waited at the end of a long, long line
for him to scribble
in our books
of his:
Toombs shot shit/
    Alaskan bars they both new
Roman boasted permaculture
    anarchism
Dan bowed/ hands clasped
    in thanks
I handed him, *The Back Country*, to scrawl upon with hands
    that've written atlatls
        clean through
mastodon, sharp tippt—
        saber tootht.
You are   the only one
who brought me   this book
tonight.

I found it in West Yellowstone, I told him.
West Yellowstone, he nodded,

    lucid:

For B.J.

Main Street Blues

Is that you, Fox?
        Bouncing above the grass blades
                and disappeared down?

Frantic?   Lost?
       Gone right/gone left and
           disappeared down
               in the waistblade grass
               and gone, under this dark
               wooded lot that the town's
               left uncut?

They'll be by
soon enough   with the tractor   again
       in a big green blaze, shave the land down dead

       and bare the squirrel-bird-coon
               possum-alleycat-cove
               and the black trash creek—
           east of the carwash
           west of the dairy queen.

Is that you, Fox?
        In dark orange and down—
            your jump   glide   step   and jump and glide
                                    down—
               still as the small   nighttime town?
Looking back toward the path you took
to get where you are.
Is that you, Fox? Gone!
Back the way you came.

Notes

Tuckasee refers to the western Kentucky and western Tennessee region of the United States.

"Energy Lake" is for my grandparents: Roy Glen Wilson of Smithland, Kentucky, and Iona Ziff Hill Wilson of Grand Rivers, Kentucky.

"Black Puma" is for Earl Atkinson.

"For Snyder" is for Gary.

B.J. Wilson is from Louisville, Kentucky. Before earning his MFA from Eastern Kentucky University, he studied literature and creative writing at Murray State University where he earned his BA and MA. Prior to declaring a major in English, he studied wildlife biology, working first at the Kentucky Dam Village State Resort Park campground and later as an amateur naturalist and pool operator at Kenlake State Resort Park. B.J. also worked as a field assistant at the Land Between the Lakes National Recreation Area in Kentucky and the Hatchie National Wildlife Refuge in Tennessee. He is the author of two collections of poetry, the chapbook, *Tuckasee*, and the full collection, *Naming the Trees,* which is forthcoming from The Main Street Rag Press. His poems appear in or are forthcoming from *Exit 7, Frogpond, Gravel, The Heartland Review, The Louisville Review, New Madrid, Tar River Poetry, Shark Reef, Valley Voices: A Literary Review* and elsewhere. He is also a musician and vocalist and his projects are available for free on his website bjwilsonpoet.com

www.ingramcontent.com/pod-product-compliance
Lightning Source LLC
LaVergne TN
LVHW041514070426
835507LV00012B/1566